Front cover – Snowboarding at Mt Hutt Skifield, Canterbury. (Andris Apse)
Front endpapers – The Shotover Jet boat negotiates a winding, narrow passage of the Shotover River, Queenstown. (Gaylene Earl, Focus NZ)
Previous page – A skier rises to the challenge and sends a shower of powder snow at the Ohau Skifield, South Canterbury. (Andris Apse)
Opposite – Dolphins play around a tour boat off the Kaikoura Coast. (Photobank)
Overleaf – Fly fishing for trout at Lake Onslow, Central Otago. (Andris Apse)

ISBN 1-86958-138-5

© 1995 Moa Beckett Publishers Limited

Published in 1995 by Hodder Moa Beckett Publishers Limited
[a member of the Hodder Headline Group]
28 Poland Road, Glenfield, Auckland, New Zealand

Printed through Bookbuilders, Hong Kong

NEW ZEALAND
ADVENTURE PARADISE

HODDER MOA BECKETT

NEW ZEALAND

ADVENTURE PARADISE

New Zealand is well-known as a scenic wonderland and the added attraction of its varied and spectacular landscape is the wide range of exciting leisure activities that are available. Picturesque mountain peaks are great to look at but they offer more than just a visual thrill – they provide some of the best skiing and snowboarding fields in the world, and challenge even the most experienced mountain climbers.

The country's rivers, lakes, large wilderness areas, glaciers, caves and beaches answer the dreams of enthusiasts of many sports. And there's plenty to delight the uninitiated too – from the adrenalin-pumping leap of faith when bungy jumping, to the sensational thrill of swimming among dolphins or speeding along a beautiful river in a jet boat.

And nothing can rival the unique view of the country that adventurers enjoy – the silver thread of a river far below while paragliding, the beauty of a clear stream while walking one of the famous national park tracks, or the mystery of exploring a cave deep underground.

These experiences are truly special and help to make New Zealand a real land of adventure.

Previous page: Aoraki Balloon Safaris flying over the tapestry of fields in the Canterbury Plains, with Mt Hutt centre right. (Andris Apse)

Climbers ascend a snow ridge on the Upper Fox Glacier at sunset. (Andris Apse)

An angler has his camp fire at the ready to cook his catch as he fly fishes for trout at sunset on the shores of Lake Brunner, Westland. (Andris Apse)

Overleaf: A bungy jumper plunges off the Kawarau Bridge towards the icy waters of the Shotover River, near Queenstown. (P. Morath)

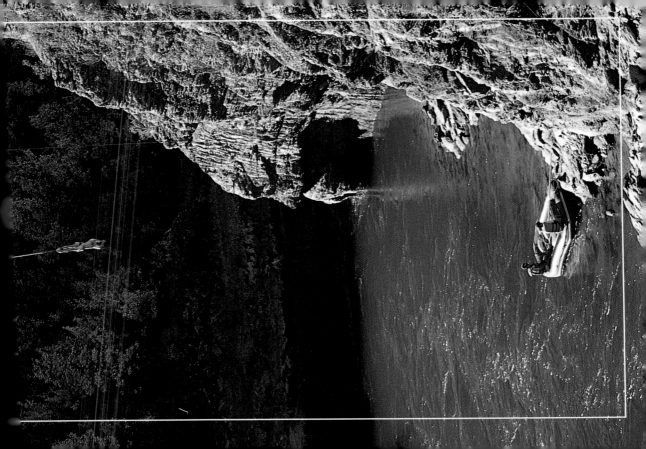

A snowboarder takes flight above the Mt Hutt skifield. (Andris Apse)

Overleaf: Paragliders suspended over the silver threads of the Rakaia River in Canterbury. (Andris Apse)

A diver has a close encounter with striped mado fish off the Poor Knights Islands. (DAC)

Overleaf (left): A Squirrel helicopter flies over mountain climbers on the Upper Fox Glacier, Westland. (Andris Apse)

Overleaf (right): The chair lift takes skiers high above Lake Wanaka at the Treble Cone Ski Field, Central Otago. (Andris Apse)

As close as you can possibly get to a dolphin – swimmers talk with the mammals. (Dennis Buurman, Focus NZ)

Overleaf: A natural ice carving – exploring an ice cave on the Tasman Glacier, Mt Cook National Park. (Andris Apse)

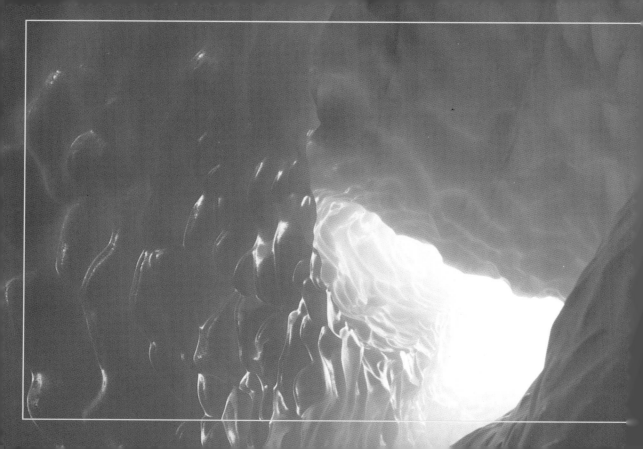

A hang glider floats like a huge bird over Rangitoto Island and Auckland Harbour.
(Photobank)

The Southern Alps provide a perfect backdrop to an Okarito Nature Tours boat as it explores the still waters of Okarito Lagoon, in Westland.

(Andris Apse)

Mountain bikers tackle the tussocky Mackenzie Country, overlooked by New Zealand's highest peak, Mt Cook. (Andris Apse)

Overleaf: A canoeist paddles through the surging waters of a boulder-strewn river in Westland. (DAC)

30

A Nimbus 3 DM glider soars above the snow-capped Puketeraki Range in North Canterbury. (Andris Apse)

A rest stop affords a spectacular view for walkers on the Routeburn Track. (B. Moorhead, Focus NZ)

Overleaf: An angler casts for trout in the clear waters of a remote stream. (DAC)

Rising above the waters of Lake Wakatipu, a paraflyer captures a bird's eye view of Queenstown. (Scenix)

Overleaf: It's all hands on deck as fishermen battle to land a marlin off the Bay of Islands. (Photobank)

Scaling the peaks of success – a climber in the Southern Alps. (G. Braun-Elwert, Focus NZ)

A sailboarder leans into the wind and skims over the water. (Fotopacific)

Walkers look down into the glassy green waters of the Arthur River from the swing bridge at Boatshed, on the Milford Track.
(Roger Fowler, Focus NZ)

Overleaf: Abseilers suspended high above the entrance to the Waitomo Caves. (Craig Potton, Focus NZ)

A jetboat speeds across the Kawarau River in Central Otago. (Andris Apse)

Overleaf: Horse trekkers on Mt Nicholas Station follow a track round the shore of Lake Wakatipu. (Andris Apse)

A humpback whale shows its tail to a group of whale watchers off the Kaikoura Coast.

(Dennis Buurman, Focus NZ)

Parapenters drift in blue skies above the Southern Alps. (Photobank)

Overleaf: A skier cuts a trail through fresh powder snow on Tasman Glacier, Mt Cook National Park. (Andris Apse)

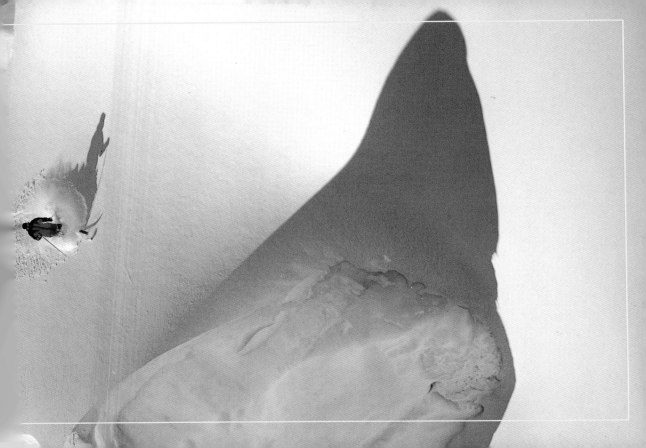

Shooting white water rapids in a rubber raft on the Shotover River, near Queenstown. (Photobank)

Overleaf: Cycle tourers enjoy an almost empty road, with Mt Cook in the background. (Photobank)

Back endpapers: Visitors lifted to the peak of Mt Fyffe by a Bell Jet Ranger helicopter enjoy the sunset over Marlborough. (Andris Apse)